INCANDESCENT

POEMS

Sibling Rivalry Press, LLC
PO Box 26147
Little Rock, AR 72221

info@siblingrivalrypress.com

www.siblingrivalrypress.com

ISBN: 978-1-943977-64-2

Library of Congress Control No: 2019936592

By special invitation, this title is housed in the Rare Book and Special Collections Vault of the Library of Congress.

First Sibling Rivalry Press Edition, June 2019

INCANDESCENT

POEMS

Kai Coggin

SIBLING RIVALRY PRESS

DISTURB/ENRAPTURE

LITTLE ROCK, ARKANSAS

FOR JOANN

CONTENTS

incandescent | ˌinkənˈdes(ə)nt |
adjective
emitting light as a result of being heated
passionate, fiery

INCANDESCENT

everything in me is a volcano
everything in me is a blazing new sun
everything in me is a conflagration of words
everything in me is a color that makes up wildfire

everything in me is a phoenix wing ablaze
everything in me is a heart's inferno
everything in me is a lucent moon
glowing
growing
giving off light
                 light
                       light
in whatever form
I can

incandescent
means
emitting light as a result of being heated

and isn't everything heated
and isn't everything ablaze
and isn't everything burning before us
and isn't the whole wide world turning to ash

can we still find the light in all that is being lost
can we still project a vision that leads humanity forward
can we still search out beauty in the rubble
can we still shine amidst the trouble
can we name ourselves luminous
and believe it
we must

we do

if you recognize this is how you move through life
you are incandescent, too

How Do You Teach Poetry?

How do you teach poetry?

You read it
out loud
to a room filled with children,

as though a fire lives in your gut,
as though magic lives in your heart,
and you only want to put it in their cupped-together hands,
you hold a magnifying glass
up to meaning,
dig around
and show them all
that
lies
beneath
until they want to find it themselves,
until they are the instigators of discovery,
until this language becomes one with their small mouths,
until they are excited in uncovering
layers of intention
and the puzzles of sounds.

How do you teach poetry?

You ask the children to read it out loud,
just a line
maybe two,

> *is that what the poet is really trying to say?*
> *are you reading the back of a cereal box?*
> *how do you think she is feeling there?*
> *remember what a metaphor is?*
> *onomatopoeia.*

and they try
and they try
and they finally break
the cusp of fear into realization,
the stage fright
becomes ownership,
they invest in the feelings themselves,
and the poem comes to life in their hearts.

How do you teach poetry?

Offer it as a safe room,
a quiet place,
a space without
teachers
parents
adults,
a sky to learn their own wings,
to fly around,
bump into walls,
soar,
hear the sound of their own inner voices,
have the freedom to truly express everything held inside,
that pain is not something they have to hold onto,
give it to poetry,
tell them

       poetry will keep your secrets,
       poetry will not leave you,
       poetry is yours, forever,

children are much deeper
than we give them credit for,
their eyes still open to the higher worlds,
their spirits still in tune with intuition
and grace,
and in this room of poetry,
in this safe carved out space,

lay a welcome mat
that starts with a smile
and
open a door
to
everything
all
at
once.

MINUS MEMORIES

Can't find my memories
years lost between birth
and moving swift across oceans at seven

from photos
I know my body was there
Bangkok
smiling girl
mother and father married
a little sister
a British school
different colored dresses
for different days of the week
gingham print yellow my favorite

in another photo
a flood
an alligator
or maybe a snake

in another photo
floating tiny candle-lighted boats
of styrofoam and banana leaf
across a swimming pool   *Loy Krathong*
festival of light
offering to the spirit of rivers—
did I float away?

in another photo
a playground
rusted monkey bars
my outstretched fingers
grassy elbows
knees

in another photo

I was a ballet dancer?

I can't put together the memories
into timeline
all shards of snapshots developed into film
shaped together hastily
to shape a childhood
no solid moments
no foundation
all fleeting
all made up from these pictures
all paper and ink
                              but no soul

how I must have felt
on the first day of school there
red lunchbox and pigtails
the look on my face
like I had already conquered kingdoms
how can I not remember
that pink dress and parasol?
the halloween costumes of cat
witch
hawaiian princess
how does dad's marine sergeant hat
slide off of my small saluting hands and head
into this abyss of blackness?

Today
I try to recall
a smell a touch
the music of a country that birthed me
across an ocean
but there is nothing
except the song on the airplane
on the way here
"all my exes live in Texas"
the universe

and
its irony

I pictured the dust
kicked up by imaginary
cowboys and horses
thought they'd be
at the airport gate in Houston
when we landed from Bangkok
minus a father
there was only a closing door
to memories
that were never really mine
to a child
who died with a different name.

I do remember his grey-brown pant-leg
my hands clutching around this tall tree of leaving
the words *take care of your mother and sister for me*
the sound of every memory before then

slipping

    away.

Becoming a Woman

The first time
I wore a dress to school
was not by choice,
a panic
implanted
by my mother,
saying I would bleed through
and it would stain my jeans,
and everyone
would know
I had become a woman.

The dress was a pale olive green,
in two drab dusky pieces actually,
a long skirt
that mocked my ankles
and subsequent vest,
twice buttoned hugging a safari-print
collared shirt,
scattered leaves patterned in a dishevel,
God,
fifth grade
didn't know
what to expect
when I sauntered cautiously into recess,
each w i d e and s l o w step,
uncomfortable mosey,
thick pad between my legs,
a mattress of distress,
and me
in a dress.

What the hell are you wearing?
my best friend Carmen asked,
and my cheeks must've
reddened

as the
crimson
visit from Aunt Flo
made her loud sanguine announcement,
ironically,
it was wearing a dress to school
that embarrassed me more than a leaked ruby
on my blue jeans could have,
well,
in retrospect,
equal embarrassment levels at least,

but alas
I endured,
and the scarlet letter Accident had been averted,
and the humid noon recess wind blew up my legs,
and my olive skirt undulated in shameful waves
by the kickball field,
and
I had become a woman.

Damnit.

I had become a woman.

THE FIRST KISS I DON'T COUNT

it's one I've never
written about
don't count
or even consider legitimate
there were no
shooting stars
weak knees
or butterflies
his mouth
a stranger
dark
the taste of metal
blood maybe
sweat
smoke of swisher sweets

13
is an in-between state
consciousness of a woman-too-soon
in the body
of a child
and
he was a stranger
who knocked on the door
and asked for a glass of water
and it was hot and it was July
and I let him inside
the house
his skin glistened like a night of stars
we sat on the couch
his name was Leroy
and he put my hands around
his hard flesh
and *Gilligan's Island* was on TV
skipper the professor too
and see
it's funny what memories do
remember only these flashes

but I can still taste
the mouth
of a stranger
and I tried to wash
the
blood
off my Winnie the Pooh bedsheets
and I ran the bathwater
over
my thighs
and something
something was broken
and it was hot and it was July

and I did not have a name for this
other
      than
        SIN

and I did not have a name for this
but this would be a silence
that would hold my tongue for years

and I don't really ever count it
as my first kiss
because so much more was taken
and he was a stranger
and it was hot and it was July
and *Gilligan's Island* was on TV

and I could not
stop crying
I just could not stop crying

the

bathwater

muffling

my loss

LANDSLIDE

sometimes
a mountaintop
misses the sea so much
she dives into the blue kiss dark abyss
without even holding her
breath

landslides are this wanting
this gravity
and reforming
and falling
in
love

reshaping the land
to join mountaintop with sea ·

my darling—landslide into me

HER

I might've been ten
when I realized
the magnets inside me
were spinning toward her
whoever *her* was
she
was my everything
my longing to be close
my ache to be seen
my dream to be kissed by
touched by
missed by
her
whoever *her* was
she
was my love
and I could not help
but be enamored.

The feelings
did not die down
they grew into silent flowers in my chest
until a meadow sprung from my mouth when I spoke
until petals only saying
she loves me
spilled from my lips and became my words
at that age I did not have the word *gay*
did not have the word *lesbian*
the word *queer* just this fear
to explain my frame of reference
around my undeniable attraction to
her.

There was always a *her*
through the years of my youth
a too-far face
I could fix my eyes and heart upon
like a star guiding me out of my blackhole secret
never close enough to touch
never close enough to whisper
never close enough to be real in my arms
I was taught those fires would burn me forever
and sin was named after a woman
but
I wanted her skin
on my mouth
so much.

The first time I kissed a girl at 17
I might have been a fault line the way I trembled
the way the earth moved all around our fresh young bodies
I remember her wild curls
falling across my face
the way she laughed the taste of her *yes*
the ceiling fan
spinning rings over our heads
and I may have never returned to earth that day
the way she sent me hovering into the atmosphere
with only the fear that this moment might not be real
and these kisses and her cheek and her neck and her shoulder
and her
and her
and her
moving up so close
to the wild magnet of me
might just be a fleeting dream
but it wasn't a dream
it was

love
real   love
my first   love
and her name stays with me
folded into my skin
and I can remember her in poems
and be right there again
two budding young flowers
opening to each others fingers
how the memories linger after 20 years
she is married now
has two beautiful children
we don't speak
and I like
to think
it is because
there is still a part of her
that remembers
how I trembled
and to no fault of hers
or mine
love sometimes
makes strangers out of lovers
but I can write her into a poem
and thank her
always
for being
real.

In Search of Salt

Butterflies
in the Amazon
drink the tears
of turtles.

This only happens
in the Amazon,
the butterflies
flutter by
in search of salt,
the turtles
oblige
with watering eyes,
open domes of sodium for the taking,
move slowly
across logs
tipped
to the mouths of rivers,
leathery wet skin dark shells
glisten in the amazon sun,
signal flash dinner bell
to floating color swarms, thirsty with need.

If you have never
seen a turtle wear a bright crown of flame
in orange and yellow butterflies,
you have perhaps
missed more in your life than you know.

There are miracles of nature
right outside your doorstep,
symbiotic relationships of hands being held
that might look like paws
or hooves,
or wings,
because nature has a way

of working together,
trees drop seeds
that feed the wild creature who
wanders the forest and squats to plant that seed
in newly fertilized ground, steaming.

The beaver dams the stream
and the salmon gather by the wall
offering their cold-slick bodies
to the black bear hungry in spring.

And outside my window a cardinal sings,
bright red flight against green,
his metallic shrill
a song from the other worlds.

The seasons revolve around an axis
that pulls us all in,
we are closer than you think,
the oneness pulses
invisibly
and you could hear it if you tried,
you could feel it in the movement of the air connecting us,
our breath all mingling in this unseen space,
I breathe you in,
and you, me,
you me we,
if you watch for the migration of hummingbirds,
if you stay silent when the wolf howls his vibration
to the fields of night,
and if you simply opened your eyes
like the turtles

you would see.

If I knew a butterfly needed my salt
in order to produce an egg,
in order to create another colorful airy winged being,

I would sit outside
and think of
all the saddest things,
or perhaps stare directly at the sun,
until I could nourish
every thirsty thing with my tears,
my face
        an open flower,
my heart
        the nectar I offer back to the earth.

ASKING PERMISSION

I consider moments,
recall magic and love that we have shared,
perhaps if I write it into a poem
it will last   forever,
perhaps energy can be pressed to paper,
light alchemized into words.

How does it feel to be formed into legacy?

Do I have your permission
to turn our lives
into a story that outlives us both?

ON BEING NAKED

I remember
the first time
my body was introduced
to the open night air
wind blowing through
a ninth-story downtown loft window
bare ass on the bottom step
up a staircase of dreams
my skin
my curves of apprehension
fat
and muscle
and goosebumps
my timid stoic shoulders
my arching back and folded arms
my tense calves and amazon thighs
my nipples firm
mouth agape
eyes reflecting Houston skyline
hair whispering with breeze
somewhere, a moon

I was always in armor   invisible now   disrobed
I carried more than the robes that I was dealt   heavy

my body
usually
uninvited
to the dance
to the table
to the dream
but this night
after you loved me

I came
dressed in a new cloak called flesh
and the wind blew
the sound of my name   *newborn*

Your Warmth

I remember a winter
when all our trees were dressed in ice gowns,
falling crowns of dripping freeze,
a mourning dove sat on a frozen branch of the oak tree
right off the back deck,
his tail feathers covered in ice and snow,
and your warmth—
that golden heart of yours
saw him in his wintry discontented shiver.

You put some charcoal on the grill
and lit a huge hot fire,
and once the smoke slowed,
you wheeled the grill close to the frozen dove
so the fire's heat could bounce off the metal roof
and melt the ice off his feathers.

Your warmth.
Your golden warmth.

This morning
you brought me outside
in the cold
to save the ladybugs,
hundreds had descended onto our house
searching for snug,
searching for corners against the wind,
now lying in red black spotted seeming death,
belly up omens of luck,
puddles of these sweet beetles underfoot,
you said
"scoop them up with this!"
you gave me a torn corner of a page,
I watched as you scooped each ladybug with the paper
and laid it into the palm of your left hand,
I followed your love-lead,
scooping,

holding my own handful of these frozen creatures
stunted by winter's approach,
twenty or so I held there in my softly closed fist,
I breathed hot breath into the hole made
by my thumb and fingers
like I do when I forget my gloves
and all of a sudden,
through this act of your warmth and love,
I felt their tiny wings and legs start to move,
little gestures of their minuscule dance,
awakening life in my hands.

We put them
in our new greenhouse,
the one we just built from antique windows
attached to the house
to protect the two hibiscus,
the jasmine,
the gardenia,
the hanging ivy,
you are always
protecting something
from the cold.

Your warmth.

Your golden heart,
how you brought me in
more than ten years ago,
and you laid me in the palm of your hand,
my tiny wings
started to move again,
awakening to life.

BLUEBIRDS RENTING THE SQUASH STUDIO

A storm approaches
dark energy
bursting
rumbling toward,
I sit outside
in my bathrobe
and wait
for the bluebirds
to return to their new house,
rent-controlled
luxury squash studio
with modern slant roof
built from a hollowed out gourd
by my love's sweet hands,
gently tied to a bend in a branch of a young ash tree.

I wait with my camera,
zoomed all the way in and hushed,
the blue pair flies from dogwood
to maple to oak and back again
circling around their
private getaway
sensing they are being watched,
I send peace,
thunder rolls.

Mother bluebird
expects children soon,
it is unclear if the eggs have already been laid
but one can sense the excitement in the air,
bright blue constant father
brings fresh worms insects,
another pine needle for warmth, another,
mother's head constantly
cuckoos out of the hole
as if to add to the grocery list while daddy runs out the door.

The chipmunk
gave them a baby shower last week,
there was cake, I heard,
sprinkled with plump spiders and seeds,
the butterflies served as decoration
fluttering their brightly colored wings,
Spring
is a time for watching everything
open up again,
the buds, the flowers—my eyes, heart.

And I write this poem
as I wait
to get the perfect photo,
the drizzle thickens,
I wonder what it sounds like
on a roof of dried squash
thup thup thup thup
the rain falls harder
everything green around us
starts to glow against the darkening earth.

My love tells me to come inside
she says that I'm making them nervous,
that the babies might be getting cold.
We make a vantage point from the kitchen window,
remove the screen
       perch
out of sight.
Bright blue father
finds the waiting branch
fluffs his wet feathers
poses for a photo
and tucks inside with mother bluebird.
Thunder rolls,
the rain falls in sheets,
all is quiet,
all is warm,
all is safe.

There's a fire burning in the fireplace,
the dogs are snoring softly,
all is quiet,
all is warm,
all is safe.

THE SAME WORDS AGAIN

I have written this poem
too many times to count,
but let this be counted,
let this too be named,
let him be counted among the night stars,
among the broken open,
what can we build from this loss?

It is hard to make the same words
sound different,
give them another song
that does not sound like blood music
on repeat,
another name,
another city,
another hashtag.

black boy.
police.
bullets.
blood.

black boy.
police.
bullets.
blood.

A corner store,
a package of skittles,
a playground and toy gun,
a wide open street in broad daylight,
a laughing mouth,
music turned up too loud,
single cigarettes,
bootleg CDs,
a broken taillight.

None of these petty details
equal the weight of a human soul.
None of these split seconds
are worth the violent theft of their names.

Today, July 13th, is the anniversary
of Sandra Bland's death in a Texas jail cell,
say her name
        Sandra Bland
say her name
        Sandra Bland
because Sandra comes from Kings,
Sandra comes from the Greek name Alexander
Sandra means *"defender of men"*
not
criminal
not
suicide in a dark prison cell
not
death by asphyxiation.

In a Facebook post she made
before her life was stolen,
she said,
"In the news that we've seen as of late,
you could stand there, surrender to the cops, and still be killed."

Be still and be killed,
rise up and be killed,
run and be killed,
all the stories
end
the
same—

be killed.

Sandra—Defender of Men,
I know you shield as many bodies as you can from the sky,
but your wings are only so long,
and every street corner spells out homicide.

How many times must your prophecy manifest
before and after your death?
In all of these myriad black forms and black faces
death by gunfire is still the outcome,
from which there is no escaping.

Another day, another hashtag.

Black lives matter.
Yes, of course all lives matter
but if black lives do not matter enough to not kill them
then clearly all lives do not matter,
so I will keep saying it:
black lives matter
Black Lives Matter
BLACK. LIVES. MATTER.

Another day, another hashtag.
I am tired of guns
finding their way into my poems,
I'm tired of my pages
turning into bodies with bullet holes torn through,
I'm tired of explaining black humanity to you.
But until you hear it, that's what I'll do.

Another day, another hashtag.
It's hard to to pull the same words
from the same bloody pool
and make these poems sound different.

Philando's name is autocorrected to *"philander"*
every time I type it,
and I go back and change it,

and I go back and change it,
because the system is designed to fail him,
the system is designed to hang him out to dry,
and I go back and change it,
because Gentle Phil was a gentle man
with a chorus of children's voices praising him,
how he knew every single one of their names,
a cafeteria full of smiling faces and hugs,
who will hold onto THAT image of a black man
and not his viral demise,
and what about Diamond?
can we talk about her strength?
can we talk about her clarity?
can we talk about her courage to live feed
a nation who has continuously not swallowed this truth:
that black men are being murdered by police at an alarming rate,
and something has got to change.

If you have been waiting for the apocalypse, this is it.
Apocalypse comes from the Greek
meaning *"to lift the veil"*
and this is what lifting a veil of ignorance looks like,
this is what conscious evolution looks like on a national scale,
this is the wheat separating from the chaff,
the grey areas of privilege finally coming to the light,
the blinders coming off of the eyes of justice,
and her scales shifting their weight finally to what looks like
Balance.

It's hard to find hope in these troubling times,
but revolution is not a quiet game,
if there were a protest here marching down Central Avenue,
I would march so loud, so strong, so proud
but there is still a confederate flag at the end of the block,
I would be chanting my little heart out
with my #blacklivesmatter sign waving boldly over my head,
but this is a quiet town,
this is not happening here, right?

this is not a big city, right?
not Baton Rouge, Baltimore, Ferguson, Dallas?
Facebook activism only goes so far,
but maybe it is a start,
and you can unfriend
but you can't unsee
real people with real hate.

You can use your power
to create safe spaces,
to validate hushed voices,
to hear the plight of a whole slice of our population
as they are screaming *"stop killing us!"*
as they have been screaming it for centuries
to deaf white ears.

It is hard to keep writing this poem.
It must be exponentially harder for a black man to keep proving

"I AM A MAN."

Maybe this poem is my protest.
Maybe my voice is louder in this quiet room.

Maybe if I hold this light up.

Maybe if we all hold our light up.

TAKE A KNEE *

for Colin Kaepernick
* sing this poem to the tune of the National Anthem

O say can you take a knee
by this game's stadium lights
oh, how proudly we've failed
all this country's black dreaming

whose broad hopes and red scars
through this perilous fight
o'er the decades we've watched
as their spirits were beaten

and the cops, they don't care,
black men murdered, it's not fair,
and though proof is found
their paid vacations are still there

O say does this black man's
peaceful protest stay brave,
how will He ever be free
if you treat him like a slave?

Surrender

it's dark
where I am
a poem feels
different
written at night
when the world outside
is more frog sound than bird
is this valley a city
of our own
sky scraping trees
the traffic hum of car-
dinals finch robin thrush the rush
of only wind through leaves not bodies
leaving home getting to point A and
be alone for a minute
sit
in the silence
of the country inside you
there is peace to be had
there is quiet
in all the noise
there are still places
where you can see the stars at night
without even trying

today we discovered
invasive
japanese honeysuckle
is spreading its red vines
has twined and swirled
around blackberry brambles
the thorny and wild
overcome
with sweet scented delicate golden birdlike blooms
fragrance catching swirls of wind

let them invade we say
let them take us both
we surrender
to beauty
any chance we get

CHANCES ARE

I went to my first gay bar
when I was 18
snuck into this 21 and up
saloon hip hop combo club
called Chances
in the gay heyday of Montrose
before gentrification
wrapped its white claws
around everything rainbow

Chances was a lesbian bar
filled to the rafters with young baby dykes
and older butches who had their lives together
gripping tight to their pseudo-wives
or lonely hearts holding hands with bud light bottles
sizing up the femmes fluttering around
like butterflies in the dark rooms
possible two step partners
late night hook ups
tender kisses in corners
hands
bodies
cheeks
hips finding a place to be safe
to move
free

at 18
I looked
like a boy
wore men's clothes
baggy pants
button up shirts
got called sir at the grocery store
filled in for my absent father as the man of the family
my hair so short that I had a fade around the sides

hiding everything female about myself
after it was taken away by the hands of a stranger at 13

I snuck into Chances
with my cool older friend Heather
using her friend's expired driver's license as a fake ID
so excited and scared but trying to act calm
nonchalant
no, I am not sneaking in
yes, I come here all the time

Joe Allen Henry was his full name
but just call me Joe
had to memorize his address
and birthday in case the cops got wise to me
my baby face brown eyes wide with
this new world of women like me
loving women like me
holding each other
laughing together
dancing in a circle around the tight dance floor
lights flashing
a disco ball
this was the nineties after all
and the closet was home to so many
not like now but back then
chances are this was sanctuary
chances are this was escape
chances are this was the only place where it was okay
for a woman to love another woman in public
the night is fuzzy now as I look back
think I might've had a beer or two
might've two-stepped to a George Strait song with a stranger
might've smiled too big that my adolescence showed
before the blue bulky butch female cop
moseyed over to me and asked for my ID

Joe Allen Henry, huh?

her badge flashed in the strobes
to the rhythm of the music
her eyes looked me up and down
my hands stuffed my pockets
head down
neck turtling into my starched collar
I was discovered
the jig was up
the man
was just a girl
trying to find a place
to dance
to be
the cop was kind to me
just shook her head and said   *you are using a man's ID?*
shame shot through me but turned to
knowing she was trying to tell me I didn't have to pretend
that the time would come and I would be myself someday
chances are she had been in my shoes a couple of decades back
chances are she knew how it felt to want to belong
chances are we had more in common
than holding the whole world heavy on our shoulders

I left without a fight
with a smile on my face
and just three years to wait
before I could come back to be safe in this space

chances are
I danced around that two-step dance floor
hundreds of times over the years
grinded my hips to other soft hips on the hip-hop side
shot pool there on Tuesday afternoons after work
always a bottleneck in my hand
cigarette smoke in my eyes
stood on the sidelines
as a woman I loved
danced with all the other girls but me

shaped my heartache into tangible numbing
learned my own ability to make a joke
to replace the rejection
chances are this place became a theater
for my splayed-out sadness
chances are I cried into my beer more times than once

there was a huge fire at Chances in 2006
the owner wanted to spend more time fishing with his son
didn't want to rebuild I heard
and everything in Montrose changed over time
there is an upscale wine bar called *underbelly*
that stands on its foundation today
gentrified all the gay away

this is a time in my life that seems so far
from who I am now
almost another lifetime
I had to be so tough
had to cling so hard to an identity
because I spent so much time in my youth hiding it
I loved someone for eight years
who never loved me enough to hold my hand
or dance with me or call me hers—at Chances

chances are it made me feel unworthy of love
chances are I thought this is the kind of love I deserved
until I met real love face to face
and the whole world became my dance floor

I cracked out of that tough boy's body
and became a woman
underneath the stars of someone who saw my light
but all these pains
were just part of the fight
the dance around the floor of my own karma
the settling of debts
from hearts I must've broken in other lives

and every heartache I remember in this life
I use as a tool to help others now

how else can we grow
from the memories that shape us?

chances are I just needed to be loved

and now I am

but more importantly

I love myself

chances are
somewhere out there tonight
there is a young girl
with a man's ID
sneaking into her first gay club
too scared to ask another girl to dance
chances are
if I saw her I would reach out my hand
pull her close
and whisper in her ear

wait
wait

it gets better, dear

SHE

She moved the hummingbird feeder
so I could see the flying red jewels through the window
with my head still on the pillow in bed.

Sometimes, the poem writes itself.

CREATING A RAINBOW
FOR THE WHOLE WORLD TO HOLD
for Gilbert Baker, June 2, 1951 - March 30, 2017

Mr. Baker refused to apply for a trademark for his creation. "It was his gift to the world," Mr. Jones said. "He told me when the flag first went up that he knew at that moment that it was his life's work."

Pull
the

r
a
i
n
b
o
w

flags
down to half-mast
pull them
from the bright blue sky
down to eye
level
and weep
a tear of thanks

look
        at the Kansas boy
        at the man
        at the queen
        at his hands
still
tinged with color

pink	*for sex*
red	*for life*
orange	*for healing*
yellow	*for sunlight*
green	*for nature*
turquoise	*for art*
indigo	*for peace*
violet	*for spirit*

our gay Betsy Ross has died

June 1978
Gay Community Center
San Francisco
Harvey Milk
asks his friend for an emblem
knows there is a movement rising
eight metal trash cans filled with rich color dye
eight huge strips of fabric each drowned in meaning
rinsed in the public laundromat late at night
evidence of dyeing
all bleached away by morning
eight stand alone colors
hand stitched together in UNION by

Gilbert Baker
say his fabulous name in thanks
Gilbert Baker

seamstress
for the cause
fabric is just fabric
until it becomes a flag
until it becomes a symbol
until it becomes a shield that
millions can throw their bodies behind

and how did he know
that these colors
later whittled down to six
because pink material was too rare/expensive
and turquoise/indigo
merged to royal blue

red   *for life*

orange   *for healing*

yellow   *for sunlight*

green   *for nature*

blue   *for harmony*

violet   *for spirit*

these six colors
would stand together
        and we would know *family*
we would see each other
        and know we were no longer alone
we would learn that over the rainbow
there would be gold
        in our friends' eyes
        in our friends' hearts
        in our lovers' unhidden kisses
        in all of us stepping out of the closet at once
        waving this RAINBOW FLAG

and when the courts finally said *yes*
and couples who'd waited decades could finally say *I do*
it was the flag they carried in their hearts
that always saw them through

Oh glorious seamstress
flag designer for Kings and Presidents
forever artist and activist
Gilbert Baker
THIS was your greatest work,

and today
we lower the
r
a
i
n
b
o
w
flag
down to half-mast
we see you eye to eye
we honor all of your flamboyant colors
we dance
we sing
we lift your name
as your spirit
rises
to
the
Pride Parade in the sky.

THE PULSE OF A RAINBOW

for the victims of the Pulse Massacre, Orlando

You might not think
such a thing exists—
       the pulse of a rainbow,
a heartbeat
made of only light
and color,
dance
expanding,
arches bending across skies,
a vibration that resonates
through time
and space
and history
and place,
but it does exist,
always has existed,
always will exist and persist through even this,
       the pulse of a rainbow.

It is a quiet pulse,
a rhythm that imbues culture,
fierce and ravishing,
soft butch
high femme
blurred gender lines
bears and queers
trans and boi and bi
every shade of a spectrum
that can't be named by naked eyes,
if only this country could hear the music
we make with our lives,
muted for so long
with the pages of an ancient book
quoted from fundamentalist cherry-picking lips,
muffled for so long

against the bigoted legislations of men,
silenced for so long
amidst the fists and rapid fire bullets of hate,
but it is still here.

The pulse.
        The pulse.
                The pulse.

The pulse of a rainbow,
always a drum,
always a pulse you can recognize
when you see another rainbow on the street dancing,
and suddenly you dance a little inside,
you shine a little brighter,
when you look into the eyes of a stranger
and know the struggle
shares your names,
when you know that this *family* is thicker than blood—
and when that innocent blood is spilled,
you feel it in your heartbeat
skipping with
the loss, the grief, the emptiness
the
stopped—
quick—
pulse—
        of a rainbow.
49 lives,
one self-loathing homophobic psychopath
opened fire and took 49 lives,
and all the colors of the rainbow
turned to red that night,
no yellow no orange no green no blue no violet
only red,
red for miles,
red flooding the nightclub,
red pumping through the music,

red spilling into the 2am Orlando streets,
red becoming the air, the walls, the building,
red mingling with other reds
until just heaps
of
fallen
rainbows
lay there in the wake
of one man's slaughter wet-dream,
a dance floor becomes a sea
of bodies and blood ankle deep,
a tomb, which minutes before was
a sanctuary,
and
where does a rainbow go
when it dies?

The pulse.
        The pulse.
                The pulse.

I read the news as it comes in,
the body count growing
from 20 to 50
to 49
because we will not count him
with the innocents,
with the bright faced beautiful souls
extinguished too soon,

and I read of the silence in the dead room
turning into a cacophony of cell phones
ring-singing a song of harmonized panic
from the pockets of the slain,
and
PLEASE DON'T LET MY LOVE'S NAME
COME UP AMONG THE LIST OF THE DEAD

"pick up the phone"
"baby, please pick up the phone"
"please text me back!"
"did you get out?"
"are you ok?"
"pick up the phone"

last words
                "Mommy I love you... I'm going to die."

The sounds of 49 cellphones play a chorus of grief,
their interwoven songs become the music
this new flock of angels can dance to
as they leave their earthly bodies,
rise as souls, still dancing,
always dancing
always laughing, singing,
doing what rainbows do... shine with color.
The pulse.

I feel it stronger in me this morning,
my heart sick with grief for these strangers
that I know so well,
through the tears somehow
my colors are renewed,
infused with
the vibrant light of them,
their beautiful brown queer skin
making my skin more brown and queer in their names,
the pulse
a drum cry of grief turned power chanting
into the face of a country that does not see us until we die en masse,
a country that hashtags #**prayers** but votes for bigots,
a country that holds tighter to its guns
than it does to its gay children.

The pulse.
      The pulse.
            The pulse.

And I can't stop looking at their beautiful young faces,
can't stop reading the details about their lives,
the 49 holes left in families,
49 love stories with rewritten twisted endings,
a future wedding now a joint funeral,
the mothers,
their families and friends, yes,
but I return to the wailing howl of their mothers,
I think of my mother, how she would bawl a new ocean.

It is raining outside,
it is raining so hard the atmosphere is breaking,
candlelight vigils materialize across the country,
the President orders flags to be flown at half-mast,
        (the rainbow flag has always flown at half-mast)
bridges and buildings light up with rainbows,
spires of the tallest skyscrapers pierce the night,
the Eiffel Tower blasts colors into the sky,
unity through tragedy,
Pride getting prouder,
cries for gun control finally getting louder,
and maybe this is the tipping point
we have been waiting for,
as democrats chant *"where's the bill?"*
after a moment of silence
on the legislative floor.

How many more mass graves must we dig
with the blunt end of an AR-15?

The pulse.
        The pulse.
                The pulse.

I sit here,
safe in my home,
colors burning to write a poem.
I read their 49 names like a mantra,

say them into the air
to make them more real,
shape their beautiful syllables
with my mouth to make their loss more palpable,
repeat them for the infinite
times they will not be said aloud in the years to come,
their names become
a prayer,
a poem,
a dance to every love song ever written.

I become the pulse.
We all become the pulse.

      The pulse of a rainbow.

STAR

There is too much darkness
to shine the light of one poem
into a room
and call it hope
and call it anything but
trying to hold a star in your hand
knowing it would burn right through you.

Still,
you do.

PUSSY

It is never ok
to grab a woman
by the pussy,
the pussy does not serve as a handle,
an ergonomic handheld device
sprinkled here on this earth for men's sick whims,
the pussy is not even up for discussion here.

Actually, I have never used the word
pussy
in a poem.
Saying *pussy* in a poem is, in fact, a revolutionary act,
but the word pussy is not what is in question here,
it is the word *GRAB*,
it is the phrase *GRAB HER BY THE PUSSY*,
this act of lewd language
that is snidely passed between a macho nacho-colored
republican candidate for president of the United States
and a tv interviewer,
in the invisible locker room of
boys will be boys will be dangerous men.

Is this even real?
Somebody pinch me.
Is this a bad episode of *Big Brother*?
Who is facilitating this mockery of substance?
The dead presidents are turning over in their graves,
their dried up bones shaking dust
with the possibility of this ass clown becoming electable.
This is like a lost episode of MTV's *The Real World*,
except it was too lewd and shocking to talk about on TV in the 90s
so it is airing now,
live on the American Presidential Debates,
and it's on every fucking channel,
and oh my god
it *is* the real world.

Pussy.
The word is not my favorite,
but I will own it for this poem.
I, as a woman, can stand firmly behind that word and call it mine.
He cannot.

Look how he lurks behind Hillary,
stealthily stalking his prey,
pacing like a wild orangutan
waiting to beat his small fists on his fake orange chest
in claiming what he thinks is his,
a sexual predator
using intimidation tactics
and gaslighting.
This was not outside the bar last night
in wherever-town USA,
this was live in front of 14 million debate watchers,
and how,
how is this really America?

Why is it that the first female presidential hopeful
has to be met
with the most vile, disgusting,
lowlife scum of a man as her opponent?

As above, so below.
Microcosm, macrocosm.
Even in this case,
the universe shows the global audience
the double standard,
the sexism,
the misogyny,
he is the groping man on the subway standing too close
and she is the one he rubs his dick on—
the shivers of disgust
have made their way through all of us women.

He is not going to be President.

He is not going to be President.

Pussies against trump.

Unite.

WOMEN IN WHITE **

Women in white
rush to the polls tonight,
votes cast for the culmination
of suffrage,
of suffering,
of historical backlash
always on our burdened shoulders.

Women will vote for the first WOMAN PRESIDENT

dressed in white
        for a birth of a new beginning,
dressed in white
        for a baptism in history's tears,
dressed in white
        because it is our turn now,
dressed in white
        because despite the decades we have yet to have our say,
dressed in white
        for Susan B. and Elizabeth,
        for all the Rosies who riveted,
        for Sojourner's Truth,
        for her and her and her and her,

for the women who came before
who opened the doors of history to close the doors on *his story*
because it is time to write
                HERSTORY.

Women in white
rush to the polls tonight
because there is a chance for our voices
to finally be heard,
for Lady Liberty to not just be some girl, but the President—

MADAME PRESIDENT

for you, for me, for her and her and her.

** *53% of white women voted for trump.*

Unnatural (s)election

The day america died,
election results
proclaim the dream is broken,
the glass ceiling remains intact,
uncrackable,
solid even more now
with the thickness of the white votes
like spackle strengthening against any breakthrough,
covering the possibility of open sky,
underneath it
the progressive inclusion of light and good
crumbles into despondent shock,
silent disbelief.

trump will never be my president,
I cannot even give him a capital letter,
he is improper,
not a proper noun
to wear this crown as
the face of democracy,
—demo(n)cra(z)y.

Today,
my voice feels so small,
unheard,
trembling,
my facebook bubble of blue friends
cry in their coffee,
grieve in their posts,
drag their dropped jaws off the floors,
feel a death in the room.
Divided we fall,
divided states of america,
where are we going
when the blind and bigoted
are leading the blind and ignorant?

I'm so scared for the world.

Silent.
I am empty of poetry.

Dis-   connected.

Cannot find the silver lining
because the silver lining is a knife now
cutting the country in two.

Severed.

America the beautiful,
I cannot see you.

Lamplight of Liberty,
Beacon of Hope—

                                    now a distress call.

S.O.S.   S.O.S.   S.O.S.

World, can you hear us?

Send help.

VIBRATION
post trump election

My words
have been dormant
in this post election storm,
lying in wait
while hate
is made the new norm,
lying like soft bullets all around me,
scattered, disjoined, unformed,
the word TOLERANCE
        is hiding behind the dresser,
the word HOPE
        is lying quiet atop a laundry heap on the floor,
the word PEACE
        is trapped at the bottom of a bottle,
the word LOVE
        is the sound of a closing door.

My words are like
soft
bullets
that will never bruise,
that will never pierce through skin,
that will never call for blood,
these words
and so many others
wait like an artillery of dreams
in the moonlit minefield of my consciousness,
waiting for exposure,
waiting for me to take a step
into the unknown territory of this jilted demo(n)cracy,
and use my voice even more now for
what is good,
what is light,
what is freedom,
what is fight.

The haze is wearing off,
the smoke of disbelief,
the shock of godlessness,
a renewal of promise
made into the still-star-filled sky,
that my voice
is a weapon of beauty,
my pen is a *sword* of truth,
my hands trembling across the keys will not fail us.
WORDS, come back to me!
Let's fight together in this new revolution,
I am gathering you up,
my sweet soft bullets,
forming you into explosions of light,
into rockets' glare of blue paradigms,
into penetrating booms of grace,
into a 21-heart salute
of what can I do to make the world better today?

This is not hippy delusion;
it is the means by which to survive these next four years.
For me as a poet, it is gathering together words
and forming them
into precise vibrations of outrage and hope,
it is illuminating every act
of conscious movement toward good,
it is knowing privilege
and using it to amplify marginalized voices,
it is vigilance against all forms of hate,
it is exposing darkness
with bright magnifications of truth,
it is combating fear
with a promise to band together and fight,
it is building bridges wherever they try to build a wall,
it is protecting each other,
it is protecting our stories,
protecting our rights,

protecting our dignity,
protecting our humanity.

This is the new old america,
the united divided states,
the blood red states and borders,
the blue lighthouses of tomorrow,
our fears are continually justified,
this is a real human ache,
his rancorous rhetoric is rippling out to the masses,
the rotten stench of long-silenced hate
is coming up through the floorboards of our country,
but this is NOT our collective fate.

At least now we know the hate is still there,
we know exactly where to find it,
we can see the white robes and torches in the light of day.

Still,
there are
MORE OF US on the side of inclusion,
MORE OF US on the side of love,
MORE OF US on the side of oneness,
MORE OF US on the side of equality,
MORE OF US on side of healing the environment,
MORE OF US on the side of resistance to hatred,
MORE OF US on the side of freedom from tyranny,
MORE OF US on the side of light and beauty,
there are
MORE OF US

and we will not be silent,
and we will not bend,
and we will not stop our trajectory of spiritual evolution,
this is a mountain,
but we are ready for the climb,
we have already tasted the clouds.

Sometimes a catalyst for real and lasting change
comes in the most difficult circumstance,
sometimes it takes a rampant wildfire
to rebuild a broken house,
so today,
I renew my purpose as a poet,
I am coming out of my quiet shock and disillusion,
I am gathering up my words
and taking a step into this dark unknown,

aiming poems

forged out of invisibility and fire,
ready to light everything I possibly can
with a vibration of hope.

SWASTIKAS INTO WINDOWS

Recently
I heard
of a woman
who turned a graffitied swastika
into a window,
who connected the lines
of the hate symbol
and formed an escape route,
another thought,
a creative solution in paint.

A small hope.
A gesture against.

If only we could really open up a window,
let some blue air waft in,
see the clouds rising to remind us of our possibility,
see the flowers still in bloom though winter looms close and dark,
yes—
but I have heard too many stories
of lines that cannot be connected,
of symbols that run deeper than blood,
of hope beaten and broken
and yellow stars reminding people
of the bleakness of what may come.

There must be something we can do,
but for now,
turn all the swastikas into windows,
add the sun shining through.

Walls in Midair

in midair
the world changes
the borders close doors
the ports of entry bolt shut
for bodies
of specific brown
of particular religion
those who pray to Allah
those who pray to flee bombs
blowing up their children
those whose babies wash up
face down on distant shores
after flee by sea
becomes watery grave
home
is a word
that has lost all meaning
and
america (first)
is
no longer
land of the free
home of the brave
a tyrant
sits in his dark throne
his maniacal pen-strokes
rob dignity
pillage dreams
rape progress
lady liberty cries patina tears
a river rolls down her thin copper dress
pools over the words
"Give me your tired, your poor,
Your huddled masses yearning to breathe free"
while
in
midair
a wall is built
that will never keep us safe

IF WE COULD TURN BACK TIME / DOOMSDAY
after Cher

Good evening
from Planet Earth,
local time on the Doomsday Clock
is two and a half minutes to midnight,
midnight
is the end of humanity as we know it,
total obliteration of our little blue dot of hope,
the decimation of the human race,
by human hands,
by human bombs,
by human eyes
turning blinders to the faces of darkness,
midnight.

> *We didn't really mean to do this,*
> *we really wanna see him go,*
> *he'll keep making us cry,*
> *and baby,*
> *If we could turn back time—*
> *If we could find a way*
> *We'd take back all the votes that elected him*
> *and he'd go away....*

It's two and a half minutes to midnight.
A team of Nobel Laureates
at the Bulletin of Atomic Scientists
has used the Doomsday Clock
to track humanity's progress or lack of humanity since 1945,
when war was still fresh on our lips,
when the rise of one mustached dictator
saw the slaughter of millions,
midnight,
tick tock, tick tock, midnight,
always this looming end on the horizon,
this mushroom cloud of vaporization by fire.

If we could turn back time—
If we could find a way.

In the last 72 years,
the minute hand has inched closer to midnight,

3 minutes to midnight in 1949
      when The Soviet Union tested its first atomic bomb,
2 minutes to midnight in 1953
      when the US tested its first thermonuclear device,
      an answer in fire,

through the cold war between the US and Russia,
nuclear promises pointed cold at each other's skies.

The minute hand has swung back and forth
through the ebbs and flows of history,
the geopolitical factors that bond and break,
the hateful handful of men that hold human existence in their hands.

10 minutes to midnight in 1990
      when the Berlin Wall crumbled and the cold war ended,
17 minutes to midnight in 1991,
      Strategic Arms Reduction Treaty signed,
      Soviet Union dissolved.
This was our safest hour.
Fast forward through more swings
of humanity's minute hand fate to 2017,
where our new white house resident embarrassment
calls for a nuclear arms race against Russia,
where a white nationalist extremist is his right hand man,
where a Muslim ban that's "not a Muslim ban"
has already infuriated nations against us,
where men acting like boys showing off who's got the bigger toys
hold our collective future in their tiny hands.

      We didn't really mean to do this,
      we really wanna see him go,

he's gonna make us all die,
and baby,
If we could turn back time—
If we could find a way
We'd take back all the votes that elected him
and he'd go away….

Also swiped from the record of political truth
are the words and facts of scientific experts regarding climate change,

CLIMATE CHANGE IS REAL.
say it with me now,
CLIMATE CHANGE IS REAL.

the world temperature is heating up,
the ice caps are melting,
the oceans are rising,
it's fucking 75 degrees in January,
we have contributed to our own destruction
but any alarming preventative eruptions
from the mouths of scientists are silenced!

The Environmental Protection Agency has a
red, white, and blue flag gag order in its mouth.
The National Parks are about to be raped and drilled for OIL!
Scientists, save your research because
this orange little man is coming for your files.
He will wipe out our environment(al progress)
and fill the void with divisiveness and lies.

"Words are like weapons they wound sometimes."
We didn't really mean to do this,
we really wanna see him go,
he's gonna make us all die, and baby,
If we could turn back time—
If we could find a way.
We'd take back all the votes that elected him
and he'd go away.

If we could reach the truth,
I know just what we'd do,
we'd move back all the minutes inching closer
to save me and you...

Good evening
from Planet Earth,
local time on the Doomsday Clock
is two and a half minutes to midnight.

Moon Still

tonight
the moon
is
still
up there

the sky
still
warm
in its pale effulgence

a halo of gold
still
somehow
found a home
around her blue fullness

and though
there is so much to cry about

this world
this world
this world

our tears
are reflecting
so
much
light

Love Notes

the love notes
that she leaves me
are invisible
in that they are not notes
written with pen paper sentiment
in that they are this life
all around us
this detail we've put into shaping
the creation we have deemed
home
family
love

this morning
at my keyboard
where I go to pray
      I'll find the words to voice
           all this feeling
there
cracked open
splayed
baby blue
half a tiny eggshell hatched
from the eastern bluebird family
nested up in the hollowed out squash studio
we tied to an ash tree by the driveway
she found it outside
brought it in for me to see
this remnant
of blue birth hope
of beginning
      when so much in the world seems to be ending
of shell cracking open and becoming sky

this is the love note
she leaves me

without pen or poetics
this fragile tender thing that crumbles to touch
but through its meaning
reflects the strongest love I have ever known

I look out the window
to where the bluebirds have made a home
watch
for tiny things learning to fly
listen
for tiny songs filling the trees
wait
for tiny wings becoming the sky

WHEN THE WORLD IS A FLOOD,
WE HAVE AN ARK(ANSAS)

maybe we are all drowning somehow
and this is the Ark
that saves us
this bowl of soul and green and wood and water

we board this landlocked vessel in our most natural state two by two
our two eyes   our two ears
our two hands   our two feet
up the ramp of coupled hope and fear onto this barge of escaping
chaos for calm
the world is a whirling wanton flood
and we are somehow safe here   slowed down
awestruck by some rare beauty
rising like bright corks that bob on waves of boundless trees

look how you can still see the stars from here
how they shoot nebulas to the backs of your eyes
          —your mind unfolds a new universe

the white noise is green here
everything hum hum buzz with new life
you can hear the opening of buds and flowers
turning their cheeks toward sky

we are filled to our volcanic brims
with 4,000-year-old water from hot springs
and this too makes us float beyond gravity
          —see the boat we have built in the ethers

I can stand on this little plot of land
and feel like I own the whole world
and if I did I would give it away freely just to say

look there still are places that quiet the moonrise over mountains
there are crystals underfoot vibrating their frequencies through your soles
there are still streams that cut their own wild rush over stones
fox and frog and bluebird sing a harmony all their own

and I won't forget what I was escaping when I came here
but when I got here I knew that I was home

maybe we are all drowning somehow
and this is the Ark
that saves us
this bowl of soul and green and wood and water

PARIS ACCORD

written upon the withdrawal of the United States of America

I asked a glacier
how she was feeling about all this
and she just shrugged
her cold shoulder before

it

fell

into

the sea

WHERE ARE THE WARRIORS?

Where are the Warriors?

Maybe once you
casually gave
yourself
a name,
light bearer
freedom fighter
revolutionist
resistance leader
marching protester
not going to stand for this
a fist raised in the air
and is your fist still there?
Has it fallen to your side
limp and tired in this lie-filled
barrage of greed-blind backsliding
by this oligarch and his dark-hearted men?

Where are the Warriors?

This is not a battle cry,
this is no call to arms,
violence begets violence and
we will not bend down to meet darkness eye to eye,
we will not lower our hearts to understand congressional evils,
we fight with our Light,
we fight with our Light,
put your warrior fist in the air,
leave it there
but take your other fist and open it,
see your four fingers and thumb stretch outward with light
to the corners of our country
covered in heavy shadows,
stretch your light to
the poor,

the lonely,
the forgotten,
stretch your light
to the brown lady afraid waiting by the border
	a fence line separating her from a dream,
stretch your light
to the bullied young child about to take her own life
	because being different is harder than it seems,
stretch your light
to the black boys who need us to shield them,
	because the police have a quota to meet
	and bullets will steal them
stretch your light
to the young mother in the waiting room filled with fright
	carrying a decision to make from one horrible night,
stretch your light
to the other warriors
	because we've only begun to fight.

Stretch outward
	to the trafficked,
		to the abused,
			to the broken,
				to the silenced,

stretch your fingers
to the streams now clogging with refuse,
to the air choking on smoke from burning coal,
to the wildlife losing their wilderness,
to america out of control,
to the Standing Rock now told to sit back down,
to the whales wrapped in plastic
who thought, in the sea, they'd never drown.

My god, how this poem could last forever in its listing of need…

A trillion ton glacier just fell into the sea.

Where are the Warriors?

So much decision
falls upon the wicked,
school children can't unlearn hunger,
Warriors who marched in pink—
        take off your pink pussy hats
flip them over and
fill them
with as many sandwiches
and apples
and juice boxes you can
until that hat bulges with new meaning.
Women, we must know persistence,
we must know that the dark reign (of men)
must be met with our willingness to lead,
to run for office,
to call out the violators of goodness,
to offer a new perspective of hope,
to Mother our country
back into beauty.

Where are the Warriors?

In Alaska,
a family of bears is afraid
to tuck into a curl of winter sleep,
because it is now lawful for hunters to shoot
them while they are hibernating,
while bear cubs dream of honey and daffodils
a hunter enters their warm cave
and unloads rounds of ammunition shells
reflecting the empty shell   of his own dark heart.
I write this stanza as protection,
as the forming of my thoughts as a shield,
a force field around every warm bear cave exhaling deep sleep,
a force field around every wild fox den fresh with feisty pups,
a force field that blocks maniacal

trophy hunters shooting from helicopters,
because,
the bloodthirsty raid
the whitest
of snow,
and these words I offer as protection,
      energy follows thought
        energy follows thought
and I cannot stop thinking about
      the innocent,
      the innocent,
      the innocent.

Where are the Warriors?

      It is at every level we must rise now.

Where are the Warriors?

      We must take off our earthly disguise now.

Where are the Warriors?

      Now, more than ever, this our time to fight.

Where are the Warriors?

      In this era of darkness, let's blind them with OUR LIGHT.

WHEN EVERYTHING IS ABOUT TO BURN

I don't know
if I should write this
on a computer
typed into the void
who will find it
in all of the rubble
who will take
the time
to open
this
document
when the skies
have fallen over head
when everything
is burning
will a poem last
longer bound in paper
or screamed into the wind
and who will hear it
when we are all fire and oblivion

today
the white warmongers
dropped a bomb they call "mother"
the largest bomb ever used in combat
a bomb to outblast all bombs
a bomb on the cusp of nuclear
that would incinerate
the flesh of men rupture
the underground
topography of the earth
a bomb that will surely signal
the beginning
of an end we knew would come

today

colonialism
waved its bomb-shaped flag
pointed it into the brink of the final war
the white warmongers
released the "mother of all bombs"
because their real mothers never taught them
about life and consequences
about actions that can't be taken back

the republican party of little boys
with shiny penis-extending globe-destroying toys
must not comprehend the repercussions
of their concussive percussions into the mouths of caves
and he must have the biggest mushroom (cloud) tip   ping
the world's axis to apocalypse
he's
laughing
with chocolate cake stuck to his lips
the sugary teeth he lies through
and he doesn't even know
which country he is bombing
today
because isis is is is is anyone, everyone,
who is the same color
as OIL.

mother.
someone with a mother was decimated today
fucker.

there was something eerie
about how the clouds looked this morning
even here
she felt the dust tinged air heavy heart
we looked up at a fallout sky
without knowing
the 22,000 pounds of explosives
had torn a crater into the face of a brown country

the shock waves flying full circle
but this is the opposite of infinity
the particles of fear
penetrating
into our lungs
into our lives
creating new divisions in our cells

you think you are safe
but would you know the antichrist if you saw him?

I don't know
if I should write this
when everything is about to burn

Nuclear Ocean

North Korea fires
another
intercontinental ballistic missile
into the open sky,
it touches the lips of outer space
and swan dives back to earth
splashing into the pacific ocean.

I lie awake at night
thinking of her nuclear fallout movements,
the dance of death,
the ripples of tragedy,
undulating thoughts of detonation,
the pulsating waves permeating
everything underneath the surface of

w
a
t
e
r

the crab crouching behind a rock,
the nurse shark trying desperately to remember
how to save its own life,
the squid burrowing under bleached dead coral,
the schools of fish without a desk to duck and cover under,
nuclear ocean
laden with falling test bombs
warming
with the heated hatred of men,
the consumption of mankind.

Tonight,
I think of how she sparkles
when the moonlight hits her smooth expanse,

how she has been the road
between the islands we make of ourselves,
how everything came from
and will end
in her blue, blue body.

Blue Babies

now there are eastern bluebird babies
three open mouths
quiet with their hunger
small grey-blue heads
peering out of the hole
that is the door to the squash studio,
an emptied out gourd tied to an ash tree they call home

it's spring
and my dear one gave me
a broken blue eggshell
she found underneath the nest
today we watch from the kitchen window
as mother and father bluebird
fly
down
from their warm gourd
to pluck fat worms from the earth
they work for hours
back and forth streaks of blue against the trees
morning to evening feeding
one
two
three
chirping heads
squealing for the buffet of decadent
spiders ants beetles worms

blue unfolds daily
miracle of nature and life

soon
their eyes will open to the sky
their wings
will be more feather than tuft and downy
they will learn

f
a
l
l
i
n
g
and flying
all by our front door

what did we do to deserve this beautiful blue omen?
these five tiny souls coexisting with us
       two women and two dogs
            are we all one family now?

at night the feeding stops
we wonder how they all fit inside that tiny gourd
how they tuck and curl their five bodies in one small space
how do they sleep?
mother and father bluebird on the outsides
outstretched wings acting as blanket
snug children nestled underneath

just look at the word "nestled"
how it comes from
nest
how can humans pretend to know such warmth?

their blue breaths must be so tender
puffs
so quiet still
so pulsing soft
with blue
radiant incubation

in a squash we strung to a tree
with hopes it would become a home

Half-Life

When you are gone,
I lose my time
in the hours that blend
into sunrise,
there is a bed
holding a space
I don't want to grace
without your face there
breathing
next to me,
lying in the place that feels most
like home
because you are there
breathing
next to me,
the air that we have created around us,
this green frog-song summer wind,
sleeping the night through
folded up in origami blankets,
little dogs curling to the backs of our knees
and belly-warm caves,
this beautiful together,
this paradise grasped,
held without squeezing,
this long walk in the woods
that always leads to each other,

and when you're gone,
even for a few days,
I realize
that life
is
only
half-life
of what it is with you here,
and you are my every minute's muse,

the inspiration to my living,
and this is only half-life
even less than,
everything is quiet,
still,
empty,
and I wait to fall asleep
until the heavy lids of my eyes
can stay open no more,
the little dogs curl closer,
tuck themselves into
the backs of my knees,

and in the morning,

half a bird sings
to half the sun

and flies in circles, circles, circles

waiting for your return.

A Fifth of Your Lies
written on the 5th of July, 2017

america
last night
you blasted rockets
red glare
into the still night air
and it sounded more like bombs to me
than ever before
sounded more like a broken song
than to this country I still belong
brown woman
queer
you are no longer welcome here
and
to get through the 4th of july
I had to drink a fifth of your lies
wasted
hazy
blurred
stuttered and stirred
swallowed down
burning here in my gut
another day of the twitter troll
punching and wrestling journalists
the president has a right to attack back they say
flaunting his disgusting misogyny
it's just a joke they say
bucking to nuclear war powers like a bull in a china shop
finally someone is standing up they say
an administration built
on lies
my god
how low we have stooped from
the beacon
we once were

inverted
light

america
(becoming great again)
bringing out all this hate again
to get through the 4th of july
I had to drink a fifth of your lies
crammed down my throat despite my vote
from a mouth I despise
it smelled   like rising fear
it tasted   like defeat
and black/brown people's tears
and bright crushed cherries
how far down we have buried
our principles

words like

honor
truth
virtue
independence
freedom
liberty
the pursuit of happiness

america
(divided and breaking)
we
wave our flags
upside-down
and
watch silent
as the words
of a declaration dissipate   into   nothing
like the smoke
from the fireworks

that sound
more like bombs to me
than ever before.

PLEASE BE ADVISED

"After consultation with my Generals and military experts, please be advised that the United States Government will not accept or allow Transgender individuals to serve in any capacity in the U.S. Military. Our military must be focused on decisive and overwhelming victory and cannot be burdened with the tremendous medical costs and disruption that transgender in the military would entail." – trump's transgender tweet ban, July 26, 2017

★ ★ ★ ★

Put down your guns,
strip down
your fatigues,
reattach your blown off   limbs,
pour the foreign sand
out of your active combat boots,
unpin your purple heart
there on your chest,
for you are not welcome here.

Though your uniform looks
as sharp as the next
soldier, the top brass
on your collar shines like lonely stars,
you must fall out of the ranks
of so-called heroes
for you are not welcome here.

One year of being out and serving
without any unit cohesion issues,
no readiness faults,
no crumbling of machismo that solidifies brotherhood,
there have always been transgender soldiers,
but now there is a price tag
for heroism
that a draft dodger civilian in chief
doesn't want to pay

for you are not welcome here.

The military doesn't want
to foot the bill for your gender-reassignment
but will spend
ten times those millions on Viagra
because their erections are more important
than you standing tall as who you really are,
though you still fight,
and serve,
and salute to,
and stand for the freedoms
this country does not allow you,
for you are not welcome here.

You have likely been a
soldier since birth,
fighting a war
inside you, against the body
you were born into,
a secret mouth,
a tightly bound up chest,
your clumsy/sure feet
stealing moments in mother's high heels,
this idea of body parts
and mirrors,
and hiding,
and tucking,
and redefining,
you have life experience
in fighting an enemy closer than skin.

Maybe you finally proclaimed your own victory
and won those battles
and fighting for something
became your mission,
became your calling,
        but don't call here,

no, not this country,
not this broken america,
they do not want you anymore, soldier,
for you are not welcome here.

The motto for the U.S. Army Special Forces is
De Oppresso Liber—Liberate the oppressed—
except you, transgender solider.

The motto for the U.S. Marine Corps is
Semper Fidelis—Always Faithful—
except to you, transgender soldier.

What good are words if 140 characters
become constitution?

Please be advised.

Put down your guns,
strip down
your fatigues,
reattach your blown off   limbs,
pour the foreign sand
out of your active combat boots,
unpin your purple (broken) heart
there on your chest,
rise up out of your flag-wrapped coffin
where you died fighting
        in a military,
        in a country
        that says you are not welcome here.

ALPHABET FOR AMERICAN SCHOOLS
for the students of Stoneman Douglas High School, and all

A is for AR-15
B
C
D
E
F
G is for Gun. Gun. Gun.
      loud boom blood room
      lessons learned in school.

Alpha-BET you never thought you'd die here—not where you clicked with algebra, had your first crush, started to love poetry, finally remembered your locker combination, played the tuba, made a touchdown, forgot your homework, laughed, learned, blossomed, bloomed.

H is for "HELP! HELP US!!"
I
J
K is for Kill Kill Kill
L is for Lockdown drill

Alpha-BET you never thought becoming a teacher meant knowing how to panic-herd 19 high school children into a closet and *pray pray pray dear god pray it doesn't end this way.*

M is for Money
N is for NRA
O is a bullet-hole
P is for "Please! PLEASE DON'T SHOOT!!"

Alpha-BET the blood will never wash away from those classrooms, every lesson stained, every triggered memory blamed on this trauma that will never scrub clean, nightmare dreams running hallway screams—it shouldn't be both a war zone and a school zone.

Q is for Question their worth, America
R is for Run. Run for your lives, children!
S is for Seventeen dead
T is for crosshairs pointed at their heads
U is for United States of Guns
V is for Victims, countless in this bad dream

Alpha-BET those mothers would have kissed their babies longer,
would have traded places, would've held them tighter to their chests
and said *no baby you should stay home from school today, no baby, no baby,
stay stay stay*

W is for Why do we fail our children this way?
X is drawn on the next target's back
Y is for You know it will happen again
Z is like see—

See an alternative to this carnage
See an end to this anguish and pain
See our outrage turn to voices
See our voices turn to votes
See all the guns turning into flowers
See children laughing
See children learning
See children safe and sound in school again

No more thoughts and prayers.

A is for Action.

ME, TOO

TIME Magazine's
2017 Person of the Year
is a collection of open mouths,
the Silence Breakers,
women who started as a drip of reckoning
turned watershed flood
in the consciousness of our county.

Two little words.
Me, too.

How many millions of women said those two little words
over the course of these past few months?

A movement that revealed the dark
underbelly of a nation
built on the subjugation
of the female body.

Me, too. Me, too. Me, too. Me, too.

I have been touched inappropriately by a male colleague at work.
"Me, too," they answered.

I have been expected to take verbal sexual innuendo in a group setting
and just laugh along.
"Me, too," they spoke.

I have been backed into a corner and had the mouth/tongue of a man
shoved into my face.
"Me, too," they grimaced.

I have been catcalled on the streets and gripped my car keys tightly
between my fingers so it makes a stabbing weapon sort of blade that
I could aim for an eye of an assailant, because we have to learn clever
ways to protect ourselves.

"Me, too," they shouted.

I have trusted a male relative or family friend,
only to have that trust misused.
"Me, too," they cried.

I have been raped and told no one would believe me.
"Me, too," they whispered.

Millions of stories,
Millions of names and faces and hearts,
so much pain,
so much abuse,
so much pushed under the rug,
America's shameful status quo,
and that's just how it was,
and that's just how it is.

Until now.

Powerful men
across all fields of human endeavor
are being exposed for exposing themselves,
are losing their jobs for demanding handjobs and blowjobs,
are coping with the loss of a life's work
for groping the breasts or ass of a woman.

Moguls, Actors, Directors,
Senators, Executives, Congressmen, CEOs,
and damn it, it is about time
these men fall to their knees in public humiliation,
it is about time karma slapped them square in their faces,
let their dirty laundry stink up
Washington DC,
Hollywood,
New York City,
Ala-fucking-bama where a child predator heard "No Moore"
from sea to shining sea

let us see these men for what they really are.
I'll leave you to come up with your names for them.

There is no turning back from this.
A new level of expectation
for the treatment of women has been established.
We are finally raising the proverbial bar
and it is going to crash through that fucking glass ceiling
once and for all.

The president can apparently get away with
"grabbing women by the pussy"
but I see half the population of this country
in invisible pink pussy hats
marching
and meowing
snarling
and hissing
sharpening their claws
because these pussies are finally grabbing back.
We are coming for you, mister president.
We are coming for you.

Who out there thinks THIS is the revolution?

Me, too.

A WALL RISES

A wall rises out of the earth,
breaking the plane
of the planet into two hemispheres,
hemispheres divided into fears and more fears.

A wall rises between the wind and the trees,
all is still, nothing breathes.

A wall rises where the sun rises
over the morning horizon,
all is dark, perpetually.

A wall becomes a mountain
that reaches into the clouds,
a summit of division.

A wall rises out of water,
tsunami of mistrust and prejudice,
america cannot swim.

A wall rolls out of his mouth,
his teeth are walls,
his words are walls,
his tweets are walls,
his hands are walls,
2,000 miles of lies and lies and lies.

A handshake becomes a wall,
the fingers are concrete
steel spikes and separation.

A heart becomes a wall,
beating and beating and beating
a bloodied message.

A wall splits a woman and child,
a cage, a foil blanket,
and *donde esta mi mama?*
donde esta mi mama?

A wall flames out of liberty's torch,
the poor, tired, and huddled masses are met with
land of the wall and home of the wall.

A wall rises from the space between races,
it seems we can hardly look at each other's faces.

A wall won't fix what is already broken.

A wall won't fix what can't be spoken.

America, we are failing each other.

What happened to treat your neighbor
as though he is your brother?

In a world of walls,
be a doorway
be a ladder
be a bridge.

In a world of tearing apart,
be coming together,
be reunion,
be merging,
be hands stretching across borders open and warm.

In a world of lies,
do not hear.

In a world of hate,
do not fear.

There is darkness unveiling itself
at every corner, but you...
you are not that darkness.

Find the common thread again,
find the humanity again,
though everything looks like it is burning,
though everything looks like it is breaking.

Build.

Be the light.
Be the light.
Be the light.

Tear down every wall that keeps us from each other.

BODY AS WARSHIP
after Warsan Shire

The cannons
have fallen quiet
stilled masculinity misfiring
at the horizon
at all that named me prison
cage
misdirected rage tempered by
the silence of propeller blades
churning underwater
stealth
moving
I am a movement
of magnitude
weight

tonight the sea is a restless friend
together we rock / sway
no resistance
I move
she moves
under me
warship heavy dance
cutting waves
sending ripples that hold only
peace   now
not pieces   broken
but a whole moving wide body
my ribcage builds
the steel unsinkable frame
of what keeps on fighting (through)
I patched the holes in my side
with lace
with flowers
I am not here for your wars

though the battles
have claimed their casualties
I float   silent
lit up from the helm
anchors no longer dragging
the memories
lifted up or cast away
navigation only the stars
my metal breastbone keel bends to true north
a manifest of secrets turns to poems

body as warship
worship this body
this shrine
of unnamed heartache
no longer being the storms
for I am victorious
the radar radius of my pulse
signals infinite circles
that could reach you
if you could see in green
and hear the blip move closer... closer... closer...
my flag-tongue flapping a song of homecoming
the war is over
the war is over

this illumined bow
this stern
umbrage
casting a shadow
for mermaids to hide under
this starboard consternation hushed
by the gentle waves
lapping upon my shoulders,
push-pulling a song of becoming

Northward

there is a hemisphere
where all the warships go to die
to rebuild themselves
into steel chapels
into churches
into grateful tombs
into windmills
into birds

my compass heart spins
flutters
the sea
moves under me
undulating a new dance
the shore calls me
closer…
and closer…
          to myself

the war is over
the war is over

set me on fire

build something beautiful with my bones

She Made Our Home a Wildlife Sanctuary

I notice
I never mix up
fresh batches of sugar water for the hummingbirds,
I never toss more birdseed into the numerous feeders,
I never plant and water green things to root and burrow into bloom.

It is her toil to be in the soil like that,
for her hands to sprinkle sunflower and stir sweet nectar,
a different stage in life,
a different scope on creation,
her labor
is for all the wild things, all the growing.

Last week our house became
a certified registered Wildlife Habitat,
she even sent in approval applications to the
National Wildlife Federation
to name our home
a safe space,
a haven for hooves and wings.

We had to have food, a water source,
trees for cover, places to raise young,
other requirements that I do not even know
because she applied and I didn't,
to make our house a sanctuary for the untamed,
a forest refuge for the feral,
and her labor is for the unprotected,
for the innocent.

The fleeing deer drink from our lake
eat soft grasses from our fields,
fawn peek through morning mist,
white tails flicker between skinny pines,
purple spray paint on our property border trees
say that these acres are safe from hunters.

Every migrating species of bird
passes through the grand central station of her love here,
knowing she has the black oil sunflower, nyjer, thistle, bright
oranges, and care.

The chipmunks have tunneled
elaborate underground cities in our orchard of fruit trees.

The raccoons and squirrels
scurry in the oaks shaking branches
that wave with gratitude.

The singing red fox
hurls his love songs and croons
from a boulder here that faces the moon.

The 10,000 frog chorus
harmonizes with the whippoorwill,
fireflies blink in updrafts,
the night is always a symphony.

The government even sent a metal sign
that she nailed gently to the front of our house
a black bear in a ranger hat and the words

CERTIFIED WILDLIFE HABITAT
This property is recognized
for its commitment to sustainably provide
the essential elements for wildlife

See, all the wild wild things
have made this home,
have settled into the space our love leaves between leaves,
have claimed the paths that our feet carve from forest,
we share the air
and music
and movement
of this land

but I must admit
it is all by the labor of her loving hands,
this constant gardener bird feeder dream builder queen.

My wild wild
life
soul
heart
found refuge and safety
in her.

THE SHAPE OF OUR LIFE IS A HEART

We have carved
something beautiful
out of the land here,
out of the ways in which
we navigate our small personal earth,
the forest acres around us
shaped with our hands to form infinite paths
we walk through each day
with our little dogs,
a family unit built of our hearts and their hearts,
our hands and their paws,
symbiosis in our love language.

After the rains, we walk,
we check the level of our lake
which looks like a heart from the sky,
the water rushes in from streams on all sides
and invisibly bubbles up from the cold spring underneath,
fresh water cuts the rock and earth in escape from overflow
and we have a bridge over the sound of its pouring,
our hands reinforced rock and cement in the crevice cut by force,
the water's escaping will not dig any deeper out of the soil
because we have formed a channel for it to dance through,
waterfall of music moving through stones and crystals,
we watch how it snakes in rapids to the fence line,
to the neighbor's land and disappears.
At this first bridge on lake's edge,
the two Italian cypress trees we planted
stand evergreen and beautiful after the storm,
a reflection of us, growing.

I stack large stones like guards on our path,
somehow rocks shaped like hearts always lay where we step,
I gather them in my mind's collection,
a museum of earth poems,
the pups walk chest deep into the water

down the boulder steps we built
for swimming in the summertime,
they follow us wearing boots of water, dripping cool.

We wind around the lake and cross another bridge
surrounded by tall pines that we have watched shoot up
since they were only inches tall,
now they grace the sky.
Another moving stream to step across,
the trickle sounds of life,
ferns are unfurling here in a bouquet of spirals,
and we wait for each other,
as one dog sniffs a scent trail of deer
I take photos of some quiet beauty unraveling,
leaves shaped like hearts emerge from the wet soil,
we move through the forest always in a push and pull of together,
fluid and respecting each other's timing and purpose.

This path around the lake
connects to a new forest path we just cut through last summer,
a red tailed hawk told me the bird's-eye view is an infinity,
here is where we come to my favorite bridge,
the one she built with my little sister
to show her the beauty of creating something
with your own hands and sweat,
sawing down pines and lining them side to side
over a stream that was dry then and untouched,
she could see its possibility,
she could already hear the sound of water rushing underfoot,
and I have learned to believe in her dreams,
to envision what she can create out of nothing,
because it is always   beauty.
The pine bridge comes to life after the rains
when the dry creek bed bustles with rushing waves,
a waterfall forms over the fat roots of an oak tree
and pools in the shape of a heart by the bridge,
and I just can't make this stuff up,
a heart of water pulses
under our feet.

Winding up our path
a mossy incline of pine trees,
we come to the soft space where
the deer sleep,
our dogs
leave them love notes in fragrances,
the pines needles are soft where we walk.

Out of the forest finally
and back on our paved circle drive,
we come out to the sky again,
the sun or stars always shining hope on our shoulders,
I planted wildflowers in patches that we watch now
with patient love and anticipation,
we count the leaves
as everything daily becomes more green
and fills in the winter brown emptiness with life again,
we know every nook and cranny of this land,
every rock and tree and creature that shares this home,
the daffodils and tulips have brought their shine,
the dogwood trees are in full bloom as I write this,
goldfinch and bluebirds are at the bird feeder,
a woodpecker is drumming out a tree song,
it is raining and there is a chance of snow later today,
I am going to build a fire after this poem,
after I walk off our path in my mind's footprints
but not without first saying

thank you
to the universe,
to the hands of fate and time,
to whatever good I must have done
in all my past lives to deserve such contentment
when the world outside is so broken,

thank you
for our love
for our home
for our little dogs

and for this space we have carved out
with our hands and hearts and sweat,

so many times
we have stopped on our infinite night walks,
we have looked through the trees
to see our house lit up like a cathedral,
the constellations smiling down so brightly on our path,
and we have just held each other,
and said,

look at our home,
look what we have built with this love.

INCANDESCENT II

in my last lifetime
i swallowed
a fire
tucked its red embers
in the pocket of my cheek
and when i speak
there are still sparks
distant with righteous fury
that unbury themselves
from my underbelly
and rise to meet

flame

and when i say her name
these embers
swell with persistent heat
a dawn glinting on my teeth
burn me at the stake
of her
spine   entwine our lives
again and again in this divine
dance
of elementals and energy
our compulsion toward combustion
fire by frenzy and friction
to produce a shift in the timeline
of cosmos   ancestors and lineage
changed by our now
let her wildfire devour me
and empower me
to move more freely through this scorching earth

burning

from the inside   out

Gratitude

First, I am filled with gratitude and humbled with the love that was put into painting the cover of this book. If you know my poetry, you know that Joann has painted the cover art for both of my other books, *Periscope Heart* and *Wingspan*, and has inspired the magic in so many of the poems within them. I knew I wanted her to paint this one, but we didn't know at first how to capture "incandescent" visually. In the heart of this past winter, I was staring into the fireplace lost in thought, and I noticed Joann was looking at me looking at the fire. For two months, she didn't let me into her studio, and when the painting was done, this is the beauty that she created. She calls it *Light of a Poet*. When I first saw it, I wept. She has captured my essence in paint, captured my spirit in her masterful play of light and shadow. Look how she painted the hand, the eye, the lips. I'm blown away by it. I am forever humbled by Joann always seeing my depth and divine potential, whether my fire is low or I burn bright. Joann, I love you and I thank you, Genghis, and Layla for all the beauty and magic you bring to my life.

Thank you to Bryan Borland and Seth Pennington, my publishers at Sibling Rivalry Press for believing in the fire that this book holds, and for working with me to make it the brightest light it can be. Thank you to my mother Ester and my sister Diana for being a constant hearth of love. Thank you to Del Greer for reading this book when it was just a wild spark. Thank you to Laura Page, Jenn Givhan, Shaindel Beers, and Philip F. Clark for taking my poems into your hearts and returning with the most amazing blurbs I could've imagined. Thank you to the Wednesday Night Poetry community and the Arkansas Arts Council for giving me the space to share my love of poetry with audiences young and old. Thank you to everyone out there who has followed my journey as a poet since my baby steps and flickers of hope five years ago. I am humbled by all of your support and love. I am held by each of you.

Thank YOU, dear reader, for holding my words in your hands right now. I hope they warm you, spark you, light you from the inside. Glow.

Acknowledgments

The author would like to thank the editors and staff of the following publications, literary journals, and anthologies in which versions of these poems have previously appeared.

"Chances Are" / *Sinister Wisdom*

"On Being Naked" / *Blue Heron Review*

"The Pulse of a Rainbow" / *Crab Fat Magazine*

"Star" / *tenderness, yea*

"Vibration" / *If You Can Hear This: Poems in Protest of an American Inauguration*

"Swastikas into Windows," "Walls in Midair," and "If We Could Turn Back Time / Doomsday" / *Hidden Lights: A Collection of Truths Not Often Told*

"Paris Accord" / *Calamus Journal*

"When Everything Is About to Burn" / *Bottlecap Press*

"Creating a Rainbow for the Whole World to Hold" / *Stonewall 50*

"Body as Warship" / *Halfway Down the Stairs*

"Incandescent II" / *Cavity*

"Where Are The Warriors?" / *Elephant Journal*

"Bluebirds Renting the Squash Studio," "Love Notes," and "Blue Babies" / *Entropy*

"In Search of Salt" / *Women's Spiritual Poetry*

About the Poet

Kai Coggin is a poet, author, and teaching artist living in the valley of a small mountain in Hot Springs National Park, Arkansas. She holds a B.A. in English, Poetry, and Creative Writing from Texas A&M University. Her work has been published or is forthcoming in *Entropy, Sinister Wisdom, Assaracus, Calamus Journal, Lavender Review, The Rise Up Review, Anti-Heroin Chic, Luna Luna, Blue Heron Review, Hoctok, Yes Poetry,* and elsewhere.

Coggin is the author of three full-length collections, *Periscope Heart* (Swimming with Elephants, 2014), *Wingspan* (Golden Dragonfly Press, 2016), and *Incandescent* (Sibling Rivalry Press, 2019), as well as a spoken word album called *Silhouette* (2017). Her poetry has been nominated three times for the Pushcart Prize, as well as *Bettering American Poetry* 2015 and *Best of the Net* 2016 and 2018. Kai teaches an adult creative writing class called Words & Wine at Emergent Arts, and is also a Teaching Artist with the Arkansas Arts Council and Arkansas Learning Through the Arts, specializing in bringing poetry and creative writing to youth around the state. For more, visit www.kaicoggin.com.

About the Press

Sibling Rivalry Press is an independent press based in Little Rock, Arkansas. It is a sponsored project of Fractured Atlas, a nonprofit arts service organization. Contributions to support the operations of Sibling Rivalry Press are tax-deductible to the extent permitted by law, and your donations will directly assist in the publication of work that disturbs and enraptures. To contribute to the publication of more books like this one, please visit our website and click *donate*.

Sibling Rivalry Press gratefully acknowledges the following donors, without whom this book would not be possible:

Tony Taylor	Russell Bunge
Mollie Lacy	Joe Pan & Brooklyn Arts Press
Karline Tierney	Carl Lavigne
Maureen Seaton	Karen Hayes
Travis Lau	J. Andrew Goodman
Michael Broder & Indolent Books	Diane Greene
Robert Petersen	W. Stephen Breedlove
Jennifer Armour	Ed Madden
Alana Smoot	Rob Jacques
Paul Romero	Erik Schuckers
Julie R. Enszer	Sugar le Fae
Clayton Blackstock	John Bateman
Tess Wilmans-Higgins & Jeff Higgins	Elizabeth Ahl
Sarah Browning	Risa Denenberg
Tina Bradley	Ron Mohring & Seven Kitchens Press
Kai Coggin	Guy Choate & Argenta Reading Series
Queer Arts Arkansas	Guy Traiber
Jim Cory	Don Cellini
Craig Cotter	John Bateman
Hugh Tipping	Gustavo Hernandez
Mark Ward	Anonymous (12)